Squash in Action

Squash in Action

Jonah Barrington
with John Hopkins

Stanley Paul
London Melbourne Auckland Johannesburg

Also by Jonah Barrington

Barrington on Squash

Stanley Paul & Co. Ltd

An imprint of Century Hutchinson Ltd

62–65 Chandos Place, London WC2N 4NW

Century Hutchinson Australia (Pty) Ltd
PO Box 496, 16–22 Church Street,
Hawthorn, Melbourne, Victoria 3122

Century Hutchinson New Zealand Limited
32–34 View Road, PO Box 40-086,
Glenfield, Auckland 10

Century Hutchinson South Africa (Pty) Ltd
PO Box 337, Bergvlei 2012, South Africa

First Published as *Tackle Squash* 1977
Reprinted 1978
Revised edition 1984
First Published as *Squash in Action* 1986
© Jonah Barrington 1977, 1984, 1986
Illustrations © Stanley Paul & Co. Ltd 1976

Set in Monotype Times and Univers

Printed and bound in Great Britain by
Anchor Brendon Ltd, Tiptree, Essex

ISBN 0 09 166281 8

Contents

Introduction

It would be a happy coincidence if we could recall here that the idea for this book came to myself and my collaborator John Hopkins instantaneously, striking us like a thunderbolt as we pursued our various paths; I, in my daily preparation for the British Open. John in search of another story for his newspaper.

We can't. The idea came to us jointly borne high on a silver plate by Roddy Bloomfield, a publisher whose experience with similar tennis books convinced him that there was a successful market for just such a book on squash.

The pith of this book, its very heart, is in the sequence of photographs which, when flicked at speed, show me illustrating how to play a stroke, be it forehand or a drop or a backhand volley, from beginning to end. No other book that we know of presents what we hope to be the correct way to play the stroke so simply and vividly. Don't know where to put your left foot on the forehand drop shot? Should you wave your right hand around as you go in to pick up a low volley? The answer is simple. Look it up.

This is a book showing not immutable bronzed men, muscles flexed, in statuesquely correct positions. It is a book that shows me moving around the court. There is more life in the pictures than in most squash instructional pictures because they were shot as I played the stroke in question. My head bobs, my brow furrows; exactly what happens in a match or game. The camera doesn't lie. Not often at any rate. So what you see before you is me for better or worse and most of the time I hope for the better.

We have tried to show orthodoxy in each sequence but squash is a game of vicious movements, of leaps and darts and lunges, and the flicker sequence will thus show occasional variances from the classic positions. We don't mind that because we wanted realism. Of course, the best technical players such as the current world veterans champion, Ken Hiscoe, might make perfect models. Despite being 6 feet tall and a hefty $12\frac{1}{2}$ stone, he pads around the court stealthily and still gets lower to the ball than most. But don't forget that 30% or 40% of the other top players regularly hit the ball off the wrong foot. And even the great Ken Hiscoe transgresses from time to time.

In some of the flicker photographs and in photographs in other sections of the book you will also catch a glimpse of another person in the background. This is my collaborator John Hopkins and we hope that his presence will add credence to our claim that this is a realistic book. Too many books in our experience tend to show only one player, who is inevitably the demonstrator, and him in the ideal position on court. They tend to forget that very often neither player can get anywhere near the ideal position on court and thus they lose their validity.

The inclusion of John, a good club player, is meant to help relate what I am saying to players of his standard. It is very easy for the top professionals to see their own problems clearly but to forget that these are not the same problems that club players and even beginners face. After all, what is simple for the professional is often difficult or even impossible for lesser men. We have tried to make a marriage of the two by using me as an example for those aspiring to better things and John as an example of someone who plays only for fun and, consequently, hasn't the time to spend on his game rubbing out the kinks that have grown into his playing style over the years.

If you are particularly hawk-eyed you will notice in some of the photographs that John's grip is incorrect. It is like an axe-man's. He is holding a £40, delicately balanced, gut-strung instrument as if it was a £5 Woolworth's meat axe. He is not alone in this failing either. I dare say that the majority of club players hold the racket incorrectly. I won two British Opens with a grip of dubious parentage and then I realized that it was wrong, put myself through an agonizing three months changing my ways and finally settled for the grip on page 17.

My noble collaborator is not up to scratch in other ways, too. A tall, lean man, he doesn't bend his knees enough to get down to the ball as Hiscoe does for instance. He stretches to play his shots instead of moving forward another half pace where he would be able to hit the ball more comfortably and, probably, more powerfully. However, for the sake of realism, we have made no attempt to conceal these faults.

As I said earlier, our aim throughout was to produce a book that would appeal both to beginners and the better players. From the questions put to me when I give clinics I know that people want to know the right way to play squash. I also understand that given the limitation of having to work for a living, many club players don't want to remodel their game. They want to be advised of ways of making minor modifications that will bring major improvements. As part-time players they have every right to look for such tips.

I hope that in this book we will go some way towards helping them. I also hope that we have created a sense of movement in the flicker pictures and that the readers will be grateful to us for sparing them yet another museum-like display of inanimate photographs.

Significant changes in the rules were made in 1984, and they came into effect on 1st May 1985. They are included in chapter 10 of this book, and you should read them closely.

1. Equipment

If you were a beginner, John, I would recommend you to buy specialist squash clothing rather than tennis clothing. Squash kit is purpose built, so to speak, which means the trousers are designed not to split when you stretch for a drop shot. Often, too, they are easily washable.

As I say, if you were a beginner I would also suggest that you don't go out and blow £30 to £40 on making yourself sartorially in the First Division when your game is in the Fourth Division. If you want to then do so by all means. I am merely saying it is not necessary to do so. Just remember: the Squash Rackets Association insist that players should wear white and/or light matching pastel clothing. That means that however much you may be attached to your stripey old rugger socks and your old red rugger shirt they won't be allowed on court.

There is a good reason for this rule. It is easier to follow the flight of a black ball if it contrasts strongly with one's clothing as well as the colour of the court. And if you wear old tennis or boating shoes then their coloured soles may well leave scuff marks on the floor of the court, which make it hard to see the ball on the floor. This is the worst offence of all,

I think, because the floor of a brand new court can be ruined within a few months if people persist in wearing shoes with black, brown or any marking sole.

That is general advice. Now let me be specific. First shirts. The better squash shirts will stretch, are long enough to tuck into a pair of shorts and sometimes have different coloured collars. But plain, simple T-shirts,which are probably cheaper, are fine to start with. The same with shorts. You can get pairs with pockets or with a strip of towelling down each side for you to wipe your sweaty hands on. You can also buy perfectly acceptable pairs that do not have pockets or towelling strips and so cost less.

Nowadays there are squash socks that have thicker soles, often referred to as cushion soles, to help protect your feet from the bashing you are about to give them on court. They can be cotton and wool, wool and nylon, almost any mixture or not a mixture at all. It's every man for himself here. I can't advise other than to say that I wear one pair of woollen stretch socks. My feet are so hard now that socks don't give me much protection. In my case they are more aesthetic than functional.

There are specialist squash shoes available now. It is no longer necessary, nor particularly advisable in my view, to buy tennis shoes. They will tend to have too soft uppers that might stretch or even tear after a while. Furthermore, they don't give such good support to the feet as do sturdy squash shoes that are also designed to help grip on a wooden floor of a squash court and not a grass or hard tennis court surface. If the shoes don't fit perfectly then don't be afraid to put on another pair of socks. The important thing is to make sure your feet don't slide inside the shoes. If they do you will have blisters on your feet and you might break a few toenails as well.

In general the thing to remember when you buy clothes is to make sure that they are comfortable. The first time you play you don't have to look as if you have just stepped out of the best sports outfitters in town.

You will need a ball but the precise sort depends on whether you play on hot or cold courts. A rough guide is that the colder the courts the bouncier the ball you need. There are four types of ball all indicated by a coloured dot stamped on the ball: a yellow dot is the slowest, the type used in championships; a blue dot is the fastest and balls stamped with a red or a white dot are in between a blue and a yellow. As a beginner don't be afraid to use a white, red or even blue ball to make sure you get a rally going. Squash is hard enough without making it even harder by playing – or trying to play – with a ball that won't bounce.

Lastly a racket. The most important piece of equipment that you will buy and probably the most expensive. My advice is to buy a good strong one to start with, bearing in mind that from time to time you will accidentally swipe it against a wall. It would be a tragedy to break a £40 racket by hitting it on a side wall. It is not necessary for it to have gut stringing – the best kind in other words. Synthetic stringing is perfectly adequate and much cheaper. I prefer a wooden-shafted racket because the wooden shaft gives me more feel of the ball on the racket head. As for a grip, I suggest you find one that is comfortable. A leather grip is inclined to become slippery after a while. I prefer a towelling grip, still the most popular on the market. Towelling absorbs sweat well.

2. The Grip

I won a number of British Open championships with what I now call an incorrect grip. It took me three months to change it. If you can learn to hold the racket correctly then it should be easier for you to hit the ball correctly. A simple guide is to place the head of a racket in your left hand and offer the handle to your right hand, assuming you are right-handed. If you are like me a left-hander, then to your left hand. Shake hands with the racket handle and your hand will then be in, more or less, the correct position.

It is essential that the forefinger grips the racket handle outside the thumb and that it is not restricted inside the thumb with the three other fingers. The forefinger in this trigger position helps to maintain the balance of the racket.

Keep the palm of the racket in the heel of your hand, though I don't mind if occasionally you move your hand further up the shaft for a delicate drop shot. The correct grip with the forefinger extended will naturally be of the right strength; you won't have to grip any tighter or looser.

Most of all, be comfortable. There are good players with bad grips just as there are bad players with good grips. I want you to become a better player and I suspect that this may mean improving your grip.

The grip on the left is wrong. The index finger is too close to the middle finger. Note how the grip on the right shows the index finger curled as if around a trigger.

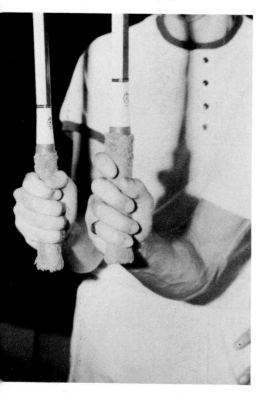

3. The Basic Strokes

The emphasis is on the footwork and the rotation of the body so that even up to impact the player retains the choice of a number of strokes – a drive, a boast for instance, even a cross-court drive. As I move to the back left-hand corner so my racket is coming up. Note how I go down, 1 to 5, to get the ball out of the corner. Notice that I put my left foot into the corner first, not, as purists maintain I should, my right foot. I believe, and so did Geoff Hunt and other

1

2

3

FOREHAND DROP

FOREHAND VOLLEY

FOREHAND BOAST

FOREHAND DRIVE

19

4

5

20

leading players of past and present, that when one is going into the forehand back corner it is essential that one leads with the wrong foot in order to make it easier and quicker to get out of the corner again. If I put my right foot into the corner first then I would probably only be able to play one stroke and that would be a boast. I don't think I would be able to swing around to play a drive. I have now pivoted and I am swinging out of the corner in 6. The racket has come through and away and I am carried through with the momentum towards the centre of the court. There is immense attention to the cocking of

6

the wrist, the bending of the legs, keeping the head down for that fraction after the completion of the stroke. That rotation out of the corner is very important. If you don't do it you will be trapped in the back corner unable to move. I play the stroke and go with it. If I had swung my left shoulder further around I would have had great difficulty in controlling the ball down the wall. The movement of the shoulder and body in the pivot must be rhythmical, not jerky.

BACKHAND DRIVE

I am advancing on the ball and preparing to play the stroke. I am not completely upright, 7. There is an emphasis on footwork. My intention is to strike the ball with the left foot forward and the right foot behind and to do so with as comfortable a stride as possible. I am getting the racket back and this is very clear-cut in the pictures just before impact. As I move in on the ball my racket goes through a movement that you could almost call a Geoff Hunt twirl though it is at a different angle. I am stretching right into the ball, 8, and taking a long stride. I am not going through too tight

7

8

to the body and as I swing notice that
my feet are basically pointed towards
the corner of the court. Because I am
going forwards I am able to open my
shoulders a little more than I would if
I was closer to my opponent and at the
same time notice that I have not swung
my right shoulder around. Notice how
high the racket travels, 9. There is
good freedom of stroke, good depth to
the drive, good bending of the knees,
balance, head down, the right shoulder
down, not lifting the head too soon. As
I complete the stroke and start to move
back to the centre of the court notice
that the racket head is up and I am turn-

9

10

11

ing my body around, 10. Notice also the emphasis I place on getting into a spring position when I have finished the stroke, 11. The wrist is cocked, which means the racket head is in a position where I can bring it up to the forehand or backhand ready for the next stroke, should there be one. From the beginning the eyes have been following the ball.

FOREHAND VOLLEY

I am just behind the centre of the court. I have followed the course of the ball through and as I have assessed what it is doing so I am starting to move to the left with the racket in position. I am moving forward. I am not upright but neither am I crouching. I am in a position from which I can spring. Notice how closely my eyes are watching the approaching ball and the way in which the racket first goes back for preparation of the stroke, 12, and then the face of the racket gradually opens, 13, 14, 15, 16, so that at impact I will slice the ball and I therefore control it more decisively. I have my head down over the ball and I am aiming to hit it on to the front wall as low as I dare and as near to the side wall nick as I dare. My stride into the ball is quite long, 16, yet remains steady. My right arm is thrust

12

13

14

15

16

17

out and used to help me maintain balance.
It doesn't dangle by the side of my body.
Notice how the left elbow remains bent at
impact, 17, and thereafter while the
racket goes through and then up the
wrist remains almost totally cocked
throughout. After impact notice I am
not overbalancing. As I watch the ball
I am travelling back towards the centre
of the court.

BACKHAND VOLLEY

I am poised just behind the T. This is a
good position. I am crouched, ready to
spring and the racket is in a position so

30

18

that I can move it from one side to the other, 18. Note how in 19 I am starting to draw my racket back. It is very apparent that I am going to have to go upwards towards the ball and in 20 I am beginning to stretch out. Again there is this attention to detail, watching the ball, keeping the racket head up, stretching across. It is essential not to overbalance on this stroke. They say volley at all costs. I don't entirely agree. Volley providing you can volley to a purpose. If you are going to stretch across, bury your knees and your nose in the wall, then it would be better to let the ball go to the back of

19

the court and dig it out from there. Having watched the ball I am coming on to it. Notice I have bent my legs. I am not arriving at the ball in a martial position. I am almost going off the ground, 22, though that doesn't happen too often. On 21 I am getting my racket back stretching upwards across court. You can see the legs working on this one. The stretch remains controlled throughout. Notice that I am up on my toes and from then on I am fully extended without taking off. The limit of my stroke can be seen on 23. I seem to have a lot more flexibility and I could be playing two types of volley. I

32

20

could be playing deep down the wall or I could be playing a short kill. I've got the racket right back, especially in 21 – it's almost sloping down on a line through my shoulders down to the floor. Then I start bringing it through again with a cocked wrist and taking it wide, 22. Notice that the wrist does not break, that the arm almost straightens at impact, 24, and not before. Notice the balance. I've gone for a short kill in the front of the court and I haven't accepted that the ball is going to be a winner and I'm balanced ready to play another shot should it happen. The racket face is slightly open at contact.

21

22

34

23

24

FOREHAND BOAST

My dreaded opponent has played a backhand stroke down the wall but the ball is running short and not to a length. I am coming forwards from behind the T, assessing the possibilities and with my opponent trapped behind me in the backhand corner, 25, I decide to play a forehand boast that will take the ball and my opponent to his front forehand corner, making him run diagonally across court. In 26, I have trailed the racket head well back to keep my opponent guessing. Although I am square to the side wall it is not until 27, which is impact, that I reveal my true intentions. He only begins to

25

26

27

move at the time I make impact, which leaves him precious little time to cover the length of the court. The angle of my body to the side wall has allowed me to angle the ball and the racket has followed through on the line of the body as well and is slightly open at impact. I have sliced the ball into the side wall, which gives me more control, though many players favour a flat, hard-hit stroke with less margin of error. As the ball moves to the far corner my body gradually swings around, the racket remains well up, the wrist is cocked and I can easily take the centre of the court. Throughout the stroke I have maintained the initiative forcing him to scamper furiously from back to front. That is a situation I like.

BACKHAND BOAST

This is a very rhythmical stroke. It is essential for me as a left-hander that I don't plant my foot deep into the corner of the court and am then unable to turn on it. If I am going to play this boast I have to make sure I have got my feet positioned so I can swivel out of the corner, coming out, in effect, with the ball. An ideal time to play a backhand boast is when my opponent has overhit the ball and it is coming off the back wall. As I go back to play it, notice how I get the racket head

38

28

up and back, 28, so that I arrive at the ball ready to play a stroke. As I go back into the corner I am bending both my back and my legs. When I have got my balance and I start to swivel, 29, notice the racket head is right up. You see the body starting to move behind the ball. In 30, I am still taking the weight on my right foot but from 31 to 34 (through the course of the stroke) I transfer my weight on to my left foot, and because of this comfortable turn I am in a good position to follow the course of the ball and move easily back to the centre of the court. This boast is hit firmly and

29

30

40

31

32

41

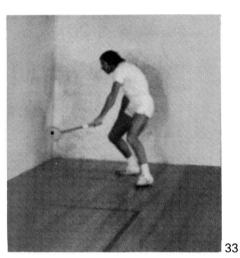

33

34

42

almost flat. I am helped in moving off the stroke by the way I have put my right foot into the corner and also by allowing the racket head to swing through and, so to speak, lead me back to the centre of the court (34).

FOREHAND DROP

I have moved off the T as I have sensed that the ball is going short. I have my racket right back again, 35, and I have my eyes trained on the ball assessing exactly where it is going. I am gradually going down to the ball and for this shot I am going to have to bend very low and

35

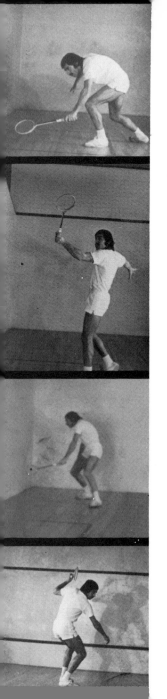

bend my back. I want to play the ball no more than two or three inches above the tin and therefore I have to get everything right. I must play the ball in an orthodox manner. If I play it off the wrong foot then I am likely to be penalized because I can't get out of the way in time. I concentrate on the ball and not on what my opponent is doing behind me. Notice in frames 36 to 41, that I come down with no wavering of the racket head and that the racket is open because I am going to slice the ball to take pace off it. I am also keeping my body clear of the ball, particularly in 40 and 41. I don't want to be too close to the ball. Having

36

37

38

39

40

46

41

gone down and played the stroke I haven't jerked myself away immediately after. The ball is coming off the side wall and if it is not hitting the nick then it is going to go very close, making a very awkward return for my opponent. I always try and make sure that I go through with the stroke. There is a tendency for the average player to let the racket drop at impact, to uncock the wrist and so flick at the ball rather than stroke it into the corner. A flick automatically means one loses control over the ball and there is far greater likelihood of the ball being scooped up on the front wall leaving your opponent with a sitter to put away.

BACKHAND DROP

This is my favourite stroke and here I am able to play it in an ideal position from near the short line. I have made a comfortable approach to the ball and the racket positions, 42–44, are ideal for early preparation. I gradually bring the racket back to its highest position, 48, and my feet are nicely in line and well balanced as I begin the stroke. You can clearly see I am transferring my weight on to the front foot for production of the stroke in 45–48, and because the ball is coming through low I have had to bend my knees and my back. The racket head becomes obviously open in 49 and from

42

43

44

49

45

46

50

47

48

51

49

50

52

there on to the end, note, the racket face is seen to be open. I hit the ball well away from the leading foot, 50, 51, and a little in front of the left foot. Tremendous emphasis is placed on the bending of the legs. My left arm is solidly planted and there is no overreaching or overbalancing. Impact is at 50. After impact through 52 the follow-through is slight. I keep my head down, my eyes follow the ball, there is no sudden twisting of the body, and finally, 53, I can start to adjust my weight and move back towards a position just near to the T (54).

51

53

52

53

54

54

SERVICE

There is one – just one – free shot in squash and that is the service. It is the only stroke you play when you have all the advantages, so force the pace. No matter how good your opponent is, he has to stand at the back of the court to receive service (see photo D on page 67). Be aggressive and always positive.

To serve an outright winner is exceedingly difficult but at worst the opponent will be placed under pressure. Hit the ball high on the front wall – just off centre, midway between the cut line and the top red line – so that it will float back to the

side wall. That will make your opponent either scramble a high volley away from the wall or, better still, let the ball go into the backhand corner. From in there, he may have difficulty in returning the serve.

Vary your serve from time to time. After innumerable high floaters toss over a hard-hit serve straight at him. See how quickly he moves.

Don't forget, if you are right-handed and playing a leftie, like me, to attack him on his backhand. I often notice right-handers continuing to serve to a leftie's forehand as though they haven't noticed that he is left-handed.

From the right box I like a simple fore-hand volley lob serve, played with my right foot forward and my left anchored in the box. From the left box I often use the same forehand lob serve. It leaves me with my back to my opponent so I usually sneak a look at him out of the corner of my eye just as I start my back-swing. Keep your swing smooth. A tennis serve will set you spinning like a top and allow your opponent to kill the ball before you can focus your whirling eyes on it.

RETURN OF SERVICE

When returning service, your main aim should be to place the ball as far away from your opponent as possible, so only occasionally play the ball short. Instead hit the ball as high as possible to the back corners – either straight down the side wall or high across court.

The correct position to take up to return service is about one foot behind the outside back corner of the service box. From this position you will be able to take the ball on the volley or you will be able to move backwards to play the ball off the back wall if necessary.

Remember, you are the receiver now, the man momentarily in the position of weakness, so be judicious and compromise. You should try and aim your returns at the back corners of the court to drag your opponent away from the centre. Then you can take over the T and dominate him.

57

4. How To Win

Jonah, I'm playing an arch rival in the semi-finals of the club championship tomorrow night. We have played each other many times so we know each other's game. We are about the same standard. How can I make sure that I beat him tomorrow night?

First, think positively. Remember the games you have won against him and not those you have lost. Be realistic. You know that the game you like to play is a game he likes to play also, so you will have to be at your best to beat him. That means cutting out mistakes, playing percentage squash.

Second, use the knock-up not as a formality but as the priceless opportunity it really is to get the feel of the ball. Don't try and hit too hard too soon. Get your swing into a groove on both the forehand and backhand. You know that he normally volleys well, but this time toss up a lob or two and see how he responds. It may be that his timing is off tonight. On the other hand, if he hits it tremendously hard into the nick then you know what shot not to play.

Third, prepare yourself for the court. Note the speed of the ball. Is it coming off the front wall faster or slower than usual? Remind yourself of the height of the ceilings, fling one high into the lights to see what sort of lighting there is. Get all this done during the knock-up. When you come to spinning the racket you are prepared for battle. So far you have just been sounding him out.

I lose the serve, Jonah. How do I start?

Pretend the first point is match point. You must have seen people playing feverishly later on in a game when they want those crucial points. They should have been playing that way from the start. You're out of hand so you want to get the service back. You're looking for length immediately, trying to push him to the back of the court so that you can then pull him to the front. Don't change the speed of a rally too soon. Don't yet go for that cross-court volley nick you've been practising. You haven't got your rhythm. Start sensibly and fight for every ball.

Nevertheless I make a bad start, Jonah. I've lost the first game. He went through me much faster than I anticipated and I am a little worried. What do I do now?

You lost it because he got in quickly, got a rhythm going. You were a bit nervy, couldn't find a length, made some unforced errors. You've got to get your rhythm and get the ball to the back of

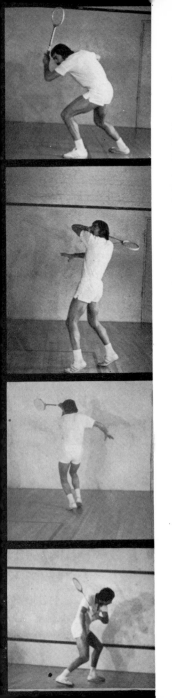

the court so that by forcing your way into a rally you can get a feel of the game. Don't be hustled. If you want to, pause for a moment before serving. Take an extra deep breath after the end of a rally as you walk into the service box. Above all play positively. Don't throw away this game with a flurry of shots off the top of your head.

If you find you are being blasted off court remember to hit the ball a little higher on the front wall, and play some lobs to break his pace and rhythm. This will prevent your opponent from having such easy targets around half court. Don't worry about losing that first game. The bloke's still got to win two more and you know that your percentage game will work, given time. Keep cool.

I was better in that game, Jonah. I got him off the T and back into the corners by hitting the ball higher as you suggested. But I still lost the game 9–5. Two–love down, what about the crucial third?

Play for time. Don't despair, because the third game is paradoxically the hardest game for him to win – subconsciously he feels he is almost home and so he relaxes. I played Geoff Hunt and lost the first game 9–3 and the second by the same margin. I was 7–0 down in the

60

third, about as near to defeat as I could get without actually losing. Then he tried some risky shots and I crept back, 1–7, 2–7, 3–7 until I won the game 9–7. I didn't lose faith in myself. I was fighting for my life, like a rat in a trap. As long as you are playing good basic sound squash he will make a couple of errors as he gets anxious to finish you off. Even if you lose 3–0 you must make him win every point in that third game. Pressure him slightly, force him further back in the court. Unless you are completely outclassed in the first two games then you will probably win the third. It's odd the way that happens but, believe me, it usually does. I've had it happen to me often enough.

Fine, Jonah, I win that game 9–4. I win the fourth too, but now I'm very tired. I've had a hard day in the office. The blister on my right hand is hurting like hell and I've had to fight all the way to get back into the game.

Stop complaining. This is mental this game. This is where you show your character. You have to concentrate more than ever. Now it's your turn to make sure that having regained supremacy you don't throw it away. Never hurry. Keep calm. Keep it simple. As your legs ache, your arm hurts, your blister bursts and oozes

61

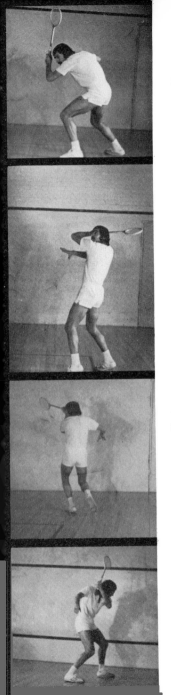

muck all over your hand, as all this happens think to yourself that it was you not he who clawed your way back from the abyss. And if you can do that then you can hold on for one more game. I always say that the start of the fifth is the start of a new match. You've come back on a radar beam to win the last two games but there is no easy way to win the fifth. You are getting more confident now, which is right. But don't forget you haven't won yet. You have just made it even steven.

It's scrappy squash, Jonah, with neither of us able to take a decent lead. Now it's 8–8 in the fifth.

At this point special tactics are called for. I don't reveal these to everyone. First you hit him with a left hook. Then you trip him with your racket. If that doesn't work, John, then start praying. Seriously, now you must not snatch at a ball. Don't rush a shot, don't crash a drive, don't attempt a delicate drop. Your heart is beating faster, your breathing is harder, everything is mitigating against delicacy.

You've gone to 8–8 in the fifth. You've worked for an hour and fifteen minutes. Why throw it away by planting the ball straight into the tin when going for a cross-court volley? Why not a straight one instead? Greatness comes out when a player is absolutely shagged yet he still plays the percentage game. At 8–8 Cam Nancarrow would try for a nick from a return of service. He would probably get it too. But that's Cam Nancarrow. For the average person I say no, don't do that. Stick with the basic, tidy, unfrilly squash that has got you to 8–8. And, John?

Yes, Jonah?

Stop complaining about your hand, your breath, your feet, your legs and your racket.

5. Problem Situations – What Do I Do Now?

A My opponent is well balanced on the T. He has drawn me up to the front forehand corner. How do I hit the ball without hitting him, Jonah, or without hitting it to him?

Answer: By lobbing straight down the nearest side wall or high across court, John. You could try a hard-hit cross-court drive.

A

B My opponent is on the T looking like a giant octopus. I am penned in the back corner. How do I get the ball out so that I have time to get out of the corner myself and can regain the initiative?

Answer: Again you must hit the ball high down the side wall, John, or high across court. But really high this time. Another possibility is a slow boast, which will take him to the front of the court where he will have to wait for the ball to land and that will give you time to come out of the corner.

B

C My opponent is right by my side at half court. How do I get him out of the way? We keep barging one another and it is getting very frustrating.

Answer: A hard drive, aimed just off centre to force him backwards to three-quarter court. Or: a reverse angle played across his body up to the front of the court. But beware of the penalty point or let in this situation.

C

D My opponent, a big, strong-armed man, constantly hurls down fast winning serves. How do I overcome them?
Answer: Do not stare at the front wall. The answer is not written there. Watch him and the ball whenever possible. Make sure your feet are properly aligned and turn your head to watch him. Don't stand too near the side wall, nor too far back.

D

E My opponent's deep drives have me in trouble in the back corners. I am afraid to go in and hit for fear of breaking my racket. Besides, I feel there is not enough room there for me to swing at the ball. What do I do now, Jonah?

Answer: A possibility is a back wall boast – hit the ball upwards on to the back wall and hope that it will carry back on to the front wall. Or try a slow high boast, as in **B**. Or shorten the grip on the racket, as Gogi Alauddin does in such situations, and hope to squeeze it out.

E

68

F My opponent's high serves just kiss the side wall. I rush forward to try and volley them, miss and by the time I have recovered the ball is past me and dying in the back corner. Help!

Answer: Move further forward, John. Threaten the server. Then you will be able to try and volley the ball before it hits the side wall and if you miss that shot then you have a second chance – when it comes off the side wall.

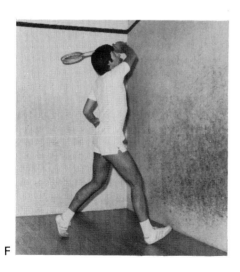

F

69

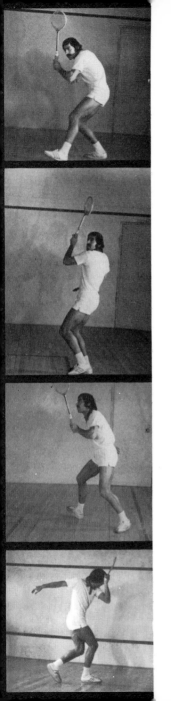

6. Joining A Club

I am anxious to play more, Jonah, but when I tried to join my local club I couldn't get in. Membership was closed they said. I rang some of the other clubs in my area but they were all full too.

I hope you put your name down on a waiting list for one of them, John. Meantime, isn't there a sports centre in your area? Most people in England have one within ten miles, according to the Sports Council. You will find a heavy demand for courts there too. But the advantage of these centres is that you don't have to be a member. You can just ring up, book a court, pay your money and then play. Consequently this form of squash is quite cheap.

I'll do that but I would still like to join a club. How much will it cost me do you think?

Depends how long the waiting list is. It won't be cheap and over a year it will certainly cost you more than at your local sports centre. Annual membership might be between £40 and £50, and court fees could be anything up to £4 an hour per person.

And how do I get some lessons?

The sports centre might well have a professional or amateur coach visiting on certain nights each week. Inquire at reception. I think you are doing the right thing if you want to join a club to get competitive squash. You will be able to play against the better club players and if you are good enough – when you are good enough – you will be able to play in club matches. Sports centres are excellent for those who just want to thrash around for exercise with a regular partner. But for competition, it's got to be a club.

You may be lucky enough to find a sports centre which runs club teams as well.

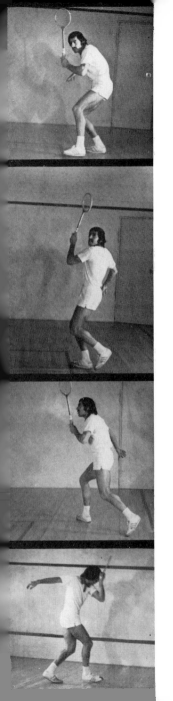

7. Training

After more than ten years and thousands of miles of running I consider myself a bit of an expert on training. Rest assured, however, I am not going to prescribe anything like my daily schedule for you.

As I see it the main problem for the average player is finding the time. I would think that most club players can manage a maximum of five hours each week in which to play and very few would want to give up any of that time to go running as well. So I shall try and outline a way for people with limited time to train and play whilst continuing to enjoy their squash.

First of all, try and get games with players who are better than you are. You will learn so much from them. Most important, you will be under pressure. Everything will seem to happen a half-second faster, but by learning to cope with a more hectic pace you will get better. Secondly, take lessons if you can. A coach should be able to pinpoint any obvious weaknesses, such as incorrect grip, and help to iron them out of your game. Thirdly, practise by yourself. Now I know this sounds very boring – and believe me I should know, after having done it for years – but it can be interesting if you know what to do instead of simply aimlessly hitting a ball around court. Half an hour each week practising alone should be enough for you soon to notice an improvement.

How many times can you hit a ball down the forehand or backhand side wall without it catching the side wall and bouncing back into mid-court? Can you stand on the T and play a drop shot into either the forehand or backhand front corners? If you can't hit a drop standing still what chance do you have when you are running? Can you hit ten successive volleys forehand and backhand on to the front wall? Better still, can you hit ten forehand and ten backhand volleys?

Another simple exercise is this: stand deep in a court on either the forehand or backhand side and hit a boast. Run up to the front and as the ball ricochets off the front wall hit a straight drive so the ball heads back down the side wall. If you boasted from the forehand corner it will be a backhand drive; if you boasted from the backhand corner then it will be a forehand drive. This will help improve your boasts and also sharpen up your footwork on your drives. If you are feeling really tigerish then see how long you can last by doing this exercise non-stop.

For variation, and to make the practice a physical one as well, do some ghosting to work the heart and lungs. Ghosting is the vile training I devised some years ago,

73

simply moving around court as in a game, sprinting to the front to play a drop, stretching to the back and leaping for a volley. The difference is that you have no opponent and no ball when you ghost. Nevertheless, pretend it is a game and if you do this hard you will find at first that a minute or so is hard work.

That's all. I did say, didn't I, that I want to provide you with a way of improving without interfering too much with your living.

8. Doubles

The doubles game of squash is an extremely enjoyable game. But I have a number of conditions that I would want satisfied before I ventured on court. By the way, the size of a doubles court is approximately half as big again (13·72 m/ 45 ft by 7·62 m/25 ft) as a singles court. You need a bouncier, harder ball to play with, too. To the best of my knowledge there are only a handful of doubles courts in Britain. Consequently 99% of all doubles games are played on singles courts.

I carry a torch for doubles because I think a proper doubles gives a player as much opportunity to think out his strokes as a proper singles; maybe more because the pressure of having two extra people on court is greater.

I should like to see the development of a new hybrid court: one of the existing 9·75 m/32 ft length of a singles court, but 2 to 2½ metres (6 to 8 feet) wider. I would use the existing ball. Such a court would be a good commercial proposition because the overheads of a doubles court are no greater than a singles court and four players can use it at once.

But that is by the way. As a game doubles is tremendously good fun for

older players who can get a sense of out-manoeuvring their rivals in a series of strokes without the frenetic physical activity necessary in singles. Doubles can be terribly skilful, fast and exciting to watch. A few years ago I played in a pro doubles tournament at Walton-on-Thames and the galleries were packed each night. Not only because there was a possibility of one of us getting a racket in our face, either.

Here I come to my first condition. I will not play doubles with anyone whom I have not seen play before. I value my head, arms, shoulders, even my ugly mug enough not to put them at the mercy of a bloke with a scything follow-through on the forehand.

My second condition is this. The game must not be allowed to become so serious that a player is tempted to play a stroke when his better judgement suggests he should take a Let. To my mind, the only way to play doubles on a singles court and, to a lesser degree a full-size court, is on the understanding that a Let is always taken in preference to a shot. It is avoiding injury again.

Scoring at doubles is slightly different. It is like American scoring in that every point won by either side is a point added to their total; instead of merely earning them the right to serve as in singles. A good thing about serving in doubles is that a double fault in singles – serving out of court, for instance – is only a single fault in doubles. I think that is good because it encourages players to attack with the service.

9. Refereeing

Nearly every club player will be aware that he or she probably does not know the rules too well. The rule about fair view and freedom of stroke is one that most club players probably don't fully understand. There is no disgrace in that. Many top-class players don't understand it either. At club level this ignorance of the rule often causes players to get in each other's way, just as they do at the game's highest level, though sometimes here it is deliberate.

The fact is, and take this as a simple guide to players and referees, that a player, having hit a stroke must then make every effort to clear out of the way. In clubs there are the half-court men, who linger around the middle of the court as if they want to buy that plot of land. Practically nothing will move them from their blessed position.

There are those who play a drop shot and then don't move away at all. They remain with their heads down, their bottoms sticking out admiring their shot. And if their opponent has to ask for a Let to avoid having to run around them they feel cheated. They are present in every club in the land.

Then there are those big swingers, the men who wield their rackets as if they

78

were throwing the hammer – enormous backswings on the forehand; long follow-throughs on the backhand.

If you have to play such a chap in your club competition the first thing to do is politely to ask him whether he would mind having a referee. If he does mind it's probably because he feels guilty and you will have to insist on one.

If you play regular competitions at your club, or if you play in the leagues, then you will come across this chap frequently. You might be prepared to risk playing him, however. On the other hand, you might be very gentlemanly, and simply politely decline to play him.

With the man who stares at the front wall you might try giving him a rap in the back as you go past just to remind him that he is in your way. But that is a fairly drastic measure. He might thump you back. It is probably better in the long run to get a referee or just to give him a miss.

As a piece of general advice for club players who are asked to referee I would insist that they first read the rules. That said they then have to rely on their common sense when they come to referee-ing. They must not assume delusions of grandeur the moment they have the power to award penalty points. I would advise almost the opposite to an in-experienced referee. I would also say that

club referees must realize that if there is any doubt in their minds then they ought to give a Let. If, in other words, they have to think for a few seconds before pronouncing then it is probably better for them to give a Let.

10. The Rules

Approved by the ISRF at its AGM in October 1984 to become effective on 1 May 1985 (but on 1 August 1985 in England).

1. THE GAME, HOW PLAYED
The game of squash rackets is played between two players, each using a standard racket, with a standard ball and in a court constructed to ISRF standard dimensions.

2. THE SCORE
A match shall consist of the best of 3 or 5 games at the option of the organisers of the competition. Each game is to 9 points, in that the player who scores 9 points wins the game except that, on the score being called 8 all for the first time, the receiver shall choose, before the next service is delivered, to continue that game either to 9 points (known as 'NO SET') or to 10 points (known as 'SET TWO'), in which latter case the player who scores 2 more points wins the game. The receiver shall in either case clearly indicate his choice to the marker, referee and his opponent.

The marker shall call either 'NO SET' or 'SET TWO' as applicable before play continues.

3. POINTS, HOW SCORED

Points can be scored only by the server. When the server wins a stroke, he scores a point; when the receiver wins a stroke, he becomes the server.

4. THE SERVICE

1   The right to serve first is decided by the spin of a racket. Thereafter the server continues to serve until he loses a stroke, whereupon his opponent becomes the server, and this procedure continues throughout the match. At the commencement of the second and each subsequent game, the winner of the previous game serves first.

2   At the beginning of each game and each hand, the server has the choice of either box and thereafter shall serve from alternate boxes while remaining the server. However if he serves a fault which the receiver does not attempt to return, or a rally ends in a let, he shall serve again from the same box. If the server does serve from the wrong box, play shall continue and the service shall count as if served from the correct box, except that the receiver may, if he does not attempt to return the service, require that it be served from the correct box.

Note to Markers   If it appears that the server intends to serve from the wrong box, or either player appears undecided as to which is the correct box, the

82

marker shall indicate to the server the correct box.

3   For a service to be good, there must be no foot-fault and the ball, before being struck, shall be dropped or thrown in the air and shall not hit the walls, floor, ceiling or any objects suspended from the walls or ceiling; it must be served direct onto the front wall between the cut line and the out line, so that on its return, unless volleyed, it reaches the floor within the back quarter of the court opposite to the server's box. Should a player, having dropped or thrown the ball in the air, make no attempt to strike it, it shall be dropped or thrown again for that service. A player with the use of only one arm may utilise his racket to propel the ball into the air before striking it.

4   A service is good when it is not a fault (Rule 4.5) or does not result in the server serving his hand out (Rule 4.6). If the server serves one fault, which the receiver does not attempt to return, he shall serve again. The receiver may attempt to return a fault on the first service and, if he does so, that service becomes good, is no longer a fault and the ball continues in play. A second service fault cannot be played by the receiver.

83

Note to Referees The referee shall decide what is an attempt to play the ball.

5   A service is a fault:

a. If at the time of striking the ball the server fails to have part of one foot in contact with the floor within the service box and no part of that foot touching the service box line (called a 'foot-fault'). Part of the foot may project over this line provided that it does not touch the line.

b. If the ball is served onto or below the cut line but above the board.

c. If the first bounce of the ball, unless volleyed, is on the floor on or outside the short or half court lines delineating the back quarter of the court opposite to the server's box.

Any combination of types of faults in the one service counts as only one fault.

6   The server serves his hand out and loses the stroke:

a. If he serves two consecutive faults.

b. If the ball touches the walls, floor, ceiling or any object(s) suspended from the walls or ceiling before being served.

c. If the server makes an attempt but fails to strike the ball.

d. If, in the opinion of the referee, the ball is not struck correctly.

e. If the ball is served onto or below the board, or out, or against any part of the court before the front wall.

84

f. If the ball, before it has bounced more than once on the floor or before it has been struck at by the receiver, touches the server or anything he wears or carries, whether the service was otherwise good or a fault.

7 The server shall not serve until the marker has completed calling the score. *Note to Officials* The marker must not delay play by the calling of the score. However, if the server serves, or attempts to serve, prior to the calling of the score, the referee shall stop play and require the server to wait until the calling of the score has been completed.

5. THE PLAY

After a good service has been delivered the players return the ball alternately until one fails to make a good return. The ball otherwise ceases to be in play in accordance with the rules, or on a call by the marker or referee.

6. GOOD RETURN

A return is good if the ball, before it has bounced more than once upon the floor, is returned correctly by the striker onto the front wall above the board, without first touching the floor or any part of the striker's body or clothing, or the opponent's racket, body or clothing, provided the ball is not hit out.

85

Note to Referees It shall not be considered a good return if the ball touches the board before or after it hits the front wall, or if the racket is not in the player's hand at the time the ball is struck, or if the ball is carried on the racket.

7. LET

A let is an undecided stroke, and the service or rally in respect of which a let is allowed shall not count and the server shall serve again from the same box.

A let shall not cancel a previous fault.

8. STROKES, HOW WON

A player wins a stroke:

a. Under Rule 4.6, when the player is the receiver.

b. If the opponent fails to make a good return of the ball, unless a let is allowed or a stroke is awarded to the opponent.

c. If the ball touches his opponent or anything he wears or carries when the opponent is the non-striker, except as is otherwise provided by Rules 6, 9, 10 and 13a.

d. If a stroke is awarded to him by the referee as provided for in the Rules.

9. HITTING AN OPPONENT WITH THE BALL

If the ball, before reaching the front wall, hits the striker's opponent or his racket, or anything he wears or carries, the ball shall cease to be in play and:

86

a. If the ball would have made a good return and would have struck the front wall without first touching any other wall, the striker shall win the stroke except if the ball, after rebounding from the front wall, strikes a side wall and the striker follows the ball round and so turns, or without so turning, allows the ball to pass around his body, in either case taking the ball on the hand opposite to that of the side wall from which the ball rebounded, then a let shall be allowed.

Notes to Referees

(i) This includes the case where the striker plays the ball behind his back or between his legs.

(ii) If the striker, having turned, or allowed the ball to pass around his body, chooses not to continue the rally due to the possibility of striking his opponent and, in the opinion of the referee, is able to make a good return, then a let shall be allowed.

b. If the ball either had struck or would have struck any other wall and would have made a good return, a let shall be allowed unless, in the opinion of the referee, a winning stroke has been intercepted, in which case the striker shall win the stroke.

87

Note to Referees Where the striker has turned or allowed the ball to pass around his body, a let shall be allowed.
c. If the ball would not have made a good return, the striker shall lose the stroke.

Note to Officials When a player has been struck by the ball as described in Rule 9, the marker shall call 'DOWN'.

The referee shall assess the trajectory of the ball and make all further decisions.

10. FURTHER ATTEMPTS TO HIT THE BALL

If the striker strikes at and misses the ball, he may make further attempts to strike it. If, after being missed, the ball touches his opponent or his racket, or anything he wears or carries, then if, in the referee's opinion:

a. The striker could otherwise have made a good return, a let shall be allowed, or

b. The striker could not have made a good return, he loses the stroke.

If any such further attempt is successful resulting in a good return being prevented from reaching the front wall by hitting the striker's opponent or anything he wears or carries, a let shall be allowed in all circumstances. If any such further attempt would not have made a good return, then the striker shall lose the strike.

88

11. APPEALS

Appeals to the referee under Rule 11 should be made with the words 'APPEAL PLEASE'.

In all cases under Rule 12 where a let or a stroke is desired, an appeal should be made to the referee with the words 'LET PLEASE'.

Play shall then cease until the referee has given his decision. If an appeal under Rule 11 is disallowed, the marker's decision shall stand. If the referee is uncertain he shall allow a let except where provided for in note to referees on Rule 11.2b. Appeals upheld are dealt with in each specific situation below.

Note to Referees Players making a pointing gesture during a rally should be advised that such action is not a recognised form of appeal.

1 Appeals on service.

a. An appeal may be made against any decision of the marker except for a call of 'FAULT' or 'FOOT-FAULT' to the first service.

b. If the marker fails to call 'FAULT' or 'FOOT-FAULT' to the first service, the receiver may appeal provided he makes no attempt to play the ball. If the appeal is upheld the service shall be a fault.

BACKHAND DROP

BACKHAND VOLLEY

BACKHAND BOAST

BACKHAND DRIVE

c. If the marker calls 'FAULT' or 'FOOT-FAULT' to the second service, the server may appeal. If the appeal is upheld, a 'LET' shall be allowed, with 'ONE FAULT' standing.

d. If the marker fails to call 'FAULT' or 'FOOT-FAULT' to the second service the receiver may appeal, either immediately or at the end of the rally if he has played the ball. If the appeal is upheld, the receiver shall win the stroke.

e. If the marker calls 'OUT', 'NOT UP' or 'DOWN' to either first or second service the server may appeal. If the appeal is upheld, a let shall be allowed.

f. If the marker fails to call 'OUT', 'NOT UP' or 'DOWN' to either first or second service the receiver may appeal, either immediately or at the end of the rally if he has played the ball. If the appeal is upheld, the receiver shall win the stroke.

Note to Referees If the marker has not called 'ONE FAULT' prior to the delivery of a second service and that service is a fault the receiver, if not awarded the stroke, may appeal that the service was a second service, either immediately or at the end of the rally if he has played the ball. If the appeal is upheld, the receiver shall win the stroke.

2 Appeals on play, other than service:
a. An appeal may be made against any decision of the marker.

b. If the marker has called the ball 'OUT', 'NOT UP' or 'DOWN' following a player's return, the player may appeal. If the appeal is upheld, a let shall be allowed, except that if in the opinion of the referee:

– The marker's call has interrupted that player's winning return, he shall award the stroke to the player.

– The marker's call has interrupted or prevented a winning return by the opponent, he shall award the stroke to the opponent.

Note to Referees In the latter case the referee shall also award a stroke to the opponent if he is unsure whether the marker's call was correct.

c. When the marker has failed to call the ball 'OUT', 'NOT UP' or 'DOWN' following a player's return, the opponent may appeal either immediately or at the end of the rally if he has played the ball. If the appeal is upheld, the referee shall award the stroke to the opponent.

Note to Referees

(i)   No appeal under Rule 11 may be made after the delivery of a service for anything that occurred before that service.

(ii)   Where there is more than one appeal in a rally, the referee shall consider each appeal in the order in which the situations occurred.

(iii) If a return is called 'NOT UP' by the marker and subsequently goes 'DOWN' or 'OUT', the referee, on appeal, if he reverses the marker's call, or is unsure, shall then rule on the subsequent occurrence.

12. INTERFERENCE

1   After playing a ball, a player must make every effort to get out of his opponent's way. That is:

a. A player must make every effort to give opponent a fair view of the ball.

b. A player must make every effort not to obstruct the opponent in the latter's direct movement to the ball. At the same time the opponent must make every effort to get to, and where possible play the ball.

c. A player must make every effort to allow his opponent freedom to play the ball.

Note to Referees The freedom to play the ball must include a reasonable backswing, strike at the ball and a reasonable follow-through.

d. A player must make every effort to allow his opponent, as far as the latter's position permits, freedom to return the ball directly to the front wall, or to either side wall to within approximately one metre of the front wall.

If a player fails to fulfil one of the requirements of Rule 12.1 (a to d) above, whether or not he has made every effort to do so, then interference will have occurred.

2   If any such form of interference has occurred, and in the opinion of the referee, the player has not made every effort to avoid causing it, the referee shall on appeal, or on stopping play without waiting for an appeal, award the stroke to his opponent, provided the opponent was in a position to make a good return.

Note to Referees In the case of Rule 12.1 the appeal must be immediate.

3   However, if interference has occurred but in the opinion of the referee the player has made every effort to avoid causing it, and the opponent could have made a good return, the referee shall on appeal, or on stopping play without waiting for an appeal, allow a let, except that, if his opponent is prevented from making a winning return by such interference from the player, the referee shall award the stroke to the opponent.

Notes to Referees

(i) A player who plays on despite interference forfeits the right of appeal concerning that interference.

(ii) Where a player's opponent creates his own interference, the referee shall rule that interference has not occurred unless the player has contributed to it.

4   When, in the opinion of the referee, a player refrains from playing the ball which, if played, would clearly have won the rally under the terms of Rule 9a or 9b, he shall be awarded the stroke.

5   If either player makes unnecessary physical contact with his opponent, the referee may stop play, if it has not already stopped, and award the stroke accordingly.

Notes to Referees

(i)   The practice of impeding an opponent in his efforts to play the ball by crowding or obscuring his view is highly detrimental to the game. Unnecessary physical contact is also detrimental as well as being dangerous. Referees should have no hesitation in enforcing Rule 12.2 and 12.5.

(ii) The words 'not to obstruct' in Rule 12.1b must be interpreted to include the case of an opponent having to wait for an excessive follow-through of the player's racket.

(iii) A player's excessive backswing may create interference when his opponent has made every effort to avoid such interference. In this case if the player appeals for a let he shall not be awarded the stroke.

(iv) When, in the opinion of the referee, a player's swing is excessive and is considered to be dangerous, the referee shall apply Rule 17.

13. LET, WHEN ALLOWED

1   A let may be allowed:

a. If, owing to the position of the striker, the opponent is unable to avoid being touched by the ball before the return is made.

Note to Referees   This rule shall be construed to include the cases where the striker's position is in front of his opponent and makes it difficult for the latter to see the ball, or where the striker shapes as if to play the ball but changes his mind at the last moment, preferring to take the ball off the back wall, and the ball in either case hits his opponent, who is between the striker and the back wall. This is not, however, to be taken as conflicting in any way with the duties of the referee under Rule 12.

b. If the ball in play touches any articles lying on the floor.

Note to Referees   Referees must ensure that no articles are placed on the floor by the players.

c. If the striker refrains from hitting the ball owing to a reasonable fear of injuring his opponent.

Note to Referees   This rule shall be construed to include the case of the striker wishing to play the ball onto the back wall.

d. As provided for in Rule 12.

e. If, in the opinion of the referee, either player is distracted by an occurrence on or off the court.

Note to Referees   This shall include the case of an obvious late call on the first service by the marker.

f. If, in the opinion of the referee, court conditions have affected the result of the rally.

2   A let shall be allowed:

a. If the receiver is not ready, and does not attempt to return the service.

b. If the ball breaks during play.

c. If the referee is asked to decide an appeal and is unable to do so.

d. If an otherwise good return has been made, but the ball goes out of court on its first bounce.

e. As provided for in Rules 9, 10, 11, 16.1, 17 and 19.5.

  In order for a let to be allowed in any of the Rules 13.1 (b to f) and 13.2e above, the striker must have been able to make a good return.

3   No let shall be allowed when the player has made an attempt to play the ball except where the rules definitely provide for a let, namely Rules 9, 10, 11, 13, 16.1, 17 and 19.5.

4   Unless an appeal is made by one of the players, no let shall be allowed except where the rules definitely provide for a let, namely Rules 9, 10, 12, 13, 16.1, 17 and 19.5.

14. THE BALL

1   If a ball breaks during play, it shall be replaced promptly by another ball.

Note to Referees   The referee shall decide whether or not a ball is broken.

2   At any time, when the ball is not in actual play, another ball may be substituted by mutual consent of the players or, on appeal by either player, at the discretion of the referee.

Note to Referees   Either player or the referee may examine the ball at any time it is not in actual play, to check its condition.

3   If a ball has broken but this has not been established during play, a let for the rally in which the ball broke shall not be allowed once either the receiver has attempted to return the next service or the server has served his hand out with that service.

4   Where a player wishes to appeal about a broken ball, the appeal must be made before the next service is returned by the receiver or, if it is the final rally of the game, immediately after the rally.

5   If a player stops play during a rally to appeal that the ball is broken only to find subsequently that the ball is not broken, then that player shall lose the stroke.

15. WARM UP

1   Immediately preceding the start of play, the referee shall allow on the court of play a period of 5 minutes to the two players together for the purpose of warming up the ball to be used for the match.

With $2\frac{1}{2}$ minutes of the warm up remaining, the referee shall advise the players that they have used half their warm up time with the call 'HALF-TIME' and ensure that they change sides unless they mutually agree otherwise. The referee shall also advise when the warm up period is complete with the call of 'TIME'.

In the event of a player electing to warm up separately on the court of play, the referee shall allow the first player a period of $3\frac{1}{2}$ minutes and his opponent $2\frac{1}{2}$ minutes. In the case of a separate warm up, the choice of warming up first or second shall be decided by the spin of a racket.

2   Where a ball has been substituted under Rule 14 or when the match is being resumed after considerable delay, the referee shall allow the ball to be warmed up to playing condition. Play shall resume on the direction of the referee, or upon mutual consent of the players, whichever is the earlier.

Note to Referees   The referee must ensure that both players warm up the ball fairly (Rule 15.1 and 15.2). An unfair warm up shall be dealt with under the provisions of Rule 17.

3   Between games the ball shall remain on the floor of the court in view and shall not be hit by either player except by mutual consent of the players.

16. CONTINUITY OF PLAY

After the first service is delivered, play shall be continuous so far as is practical, provided that:

1   At any time play may be suspended, owing to bad light or other circumstances beyond the control of the players, for

such period as the referee shall decide. The score shall stand.

If another suitable court is available when the court originally in use remains unsuitable, the match may be transferred to it if both players agree, or as directed by the referee.

In the event of play being suspended for the day, the score shall stand unless both players disagree in which case the match will start again.

2 An interval of one minute shall be permitted between games and of two minutes between the fourth and fifth games of a five-game match. A player may leave the court during such intervals but shall be ready to resume play by the end of the stated time. When fifteen seconds of the interval permitted between games are left, the referee shall call 'FIFTEEN SECONDS' to warn the players to be ready to resume play. At the end of the interval between games the referee shall call 'TIME'.

It is the responsibility of the players to be within earshot of the court to hear the calls of 'FIFTEEN SECONDS' and 'TIME'.

Notes to Referees

(i) Should one player fail to be ready to resume play when 'TIME' is called, the referee shall apply the provisions of Rule 17.

(ii) Should neither player be ready to resume play when 'TIME' is called, the referee shall apply the provisions of Rule 17 for both players.

3 If a player satisfies the referee that a change of equipment, clothing or footwear is necessary, the referee may allow the player to effect the change as quickly as possible with a maximum allowance of 2 minutes. If the player fails to return within the alloted time, the referee shall apply the provisions of Rule 17.

4   In the event of an injury to a player, the referee shall decide if it was:

a. Self-inflicted.

b. Contributed to accidentally by his opponent, or

c. Caused by the opponent's deliberate or dangerous play or action.

Notes to Referees

(i)   In 16.4b and 16.4c above, the referee must determine that the injury is genuine.

(ii) The referee must not interpret the words 'contributed to accidentally by his opponent' to include the situation where the injury to the player is as a result of that player occupying an unnecessarily close position to his opponent.

In Rule 16.4a above the referee shall require the player to continue play; or concede the game, accept the minute interval and then continue to play; or concede the match.

In Rule 16.4b above the referee shall allow reasonable time for the injured player to recover having regard to the time schedule of the competition.

In Rule 16.4c above the referee shall award the match to the injured player.

5   The referee shall award a stroke, game or match to the opponent of a player, who, in his opinion persists, after due warning, in delaying the play unreasonably. Such delay may be caused by:

a. Unduly slow preparation to serve or receive service.

b. Prolonged discussion with the referee, or

c. Delay in returning to the court having left under terms of Rules 16.2 and 16.3.

17. CONDUCT ON COURT

If the referee considers that the behaviour of a player on court could be intimidating or offensive to an opponent, official or spectator, or could in any other way bring the game into disrepute the player shall be penalised.

Where a player commits any of the offences listed in the Rules 12.5, 15.2 and 15.3, 16.2, 16.3 or the ISRF Code of Conduct (Appendix VI), the following penalty provisions may be applied:

Warning by the referee

Stroke awarded to opponent

Game awarded to opponent, or

Match awarded to opponent.

Notes to Referees

(i) If the referee stops play to give a warning, a let shall be allowed.

(ii) If the referee awards a game, that game shall be the one in progress or the next game if one is not in progress. The offending player shall retain any points already scored in the game awarded.

18. CONTROL OF A MATCH

A match is normally controlled by a referee, assisted by a marker. One person may be appointed to carry out the functions of both referee and marker. When a decision has been made by the referee, he shall announce it to the players and the marker shall repeat it with the subsequent score.

Notes to Officials

(i) Having only one official to carry out roles of both marker and referee is undesirable.

(ii) Up to 30 minutes before the commencement of a match either player may request a referee and/or marker other than appointed, and this request may be considered and a substitute appointed.

(iii) Players are not permitted to request any such change(s) after the commencement of a match, unless both agree to do so. In either case the decision as to whether or not an official is to be replaced must remain in the hands of the tournament referee or adjudicator where applicable.

19. DUTIES OF A MARKER

1   The marker calls the play followed by the score, with the server's score first. He shall call 'FAULT', 'FOOT-FAULT', 'OUT', 'NOT UP', or 'DOWN' as appropriate, and shall repeat the referee's decisions.

2   If in the course of play the marker calls 'NOT UP', 'OUT', or 'DOWN', or in the case of a second service, 'FAULT' or 'FOOT-FAULT', the rally shall cease.

Note to Markers   If the marker is unsighted or uncertain he shall make no call.

3   Any service or return shall be considered good unless otherwise called.

4   After the server has served a fault, which has not been accepted for play, the marker shall repeat the score and the words 'ONE FAULT', before the server serves again. This call shall be repeated when the subsequent rally ends one or more times in a let, until the stroke is finally decided.

5   If play ceases, and the marker is unsighted or uncertain, he shall advise the players and shall call on the referee to make the relevant decision; if the referee is unable to do so, a let shall be allowed.

Note to Markers   Markers must use recognised marker's calls including when the rally has ceased (Appendix I.2).

20. DUTIES OF A REFEREE

1   The referee shall allow lets and award strokes; make decisions where called for by the rules, including when a player is struck by the ball and for injuries; and shall decide all appeals, including those against the marker's calls. The decision of the referee shall be final.

2 The referee shall not intervene in the marker's calling except:

a. Upon appeal by one of the players.

b. As provided for in Rules 12 and 17, or

c. When it is evident that the score has been called incorrectly, in which case he shall have the marker call the correct score.

Note to Officials It is recommended that both marker and referee record the score.

d. If he is certain that the marker has made an error in stopping play or allowing play to continue, he shall immediately rule accordingly.

3 The referee is responsible for ensuring that all times laid down in the rules are strictly adhered to.

4 The referee is responsible for ensuring that court conditions are appropriate for play.

5 In exceptional cases the referee may award a stroke, a game or the match to the opponent of a player whose conduct is in his opinion detrimental to the match in progress and the game of squash in general. The referee may also order:

a. A match to be awarded to a player whose opponent fails to be present on court ready to play, within 10 minutes of the advertised time of play.

b. Play to be stopped in order to warn that the conduct of one or both of the players is leading to an infringement of the rules.

Note to Referees A referee should avail himself of this rule as early as possible when either player is showing a tendency to break the provisions of Rules 12, 16.5 or Rule 17.

1 *Definitions*

ADJUDICATOR   Responsible for the conduct of players and officials throughout the Tournament.

APPEAL   A player's request to the referee to consider an on or off court situation. 'Appeal' is used throughout the rules in two contexts:

a. where the player requests the referee to consider varying a marker's decision and,

b. where the player requests the referee to allow a let.

BOARD   The Board is the lower horizontal line marking on the front wall, with the 'TIN' beneath it for the full width of the court.

BOX (SERVICE)   A square delineated area in each quarter court, bounded by part of the short line, part of the side wall and by two other lines and from within which the server serves.

COMPETITION   A championship, tournament, league or other competitive match.

CORRECTLY   The ball being hit by the racket (held in the hand) not more than once nor with prolonged contact on the racket.

CUT LINE   A line upon the front wall, the top edge of which is 1.83 metres (6 feet) above the floor and extending the full width of the court.

DOWN   The expression used to indicate that an otherwise good return has struck the board or has failed to reach the front wall. ('Down' is used as a marker's call.)

GAME   Part of a match, commencing with a service by server and concluding when one player has scored or been awarded 9 or 10 points (in accordance with the rules).

GAME BALL   The state of the score when server requires

one point to win the game in progress. ('Game ball' is also used as a marker's call.)

HALF-COURT LINE   A line set upon the floor parallel to the side walls, dividing the back of the court into 2 equal parts, meeting the 'Short line' at its midpoint, forming the T.

HALF-TIME   The midpoint of the warm up (also used as a referee's call).

HAND   (As referred to in Rule 9.1.) A player's racket hand position in regard to its approximate location on one side or the other of his body at the moment of ball contact with the racket, a hand on the right side of his body (if facing the front wall) being right and on the left side, left.

HAND-IN   The period from the time a player becomes server until he becomes receiver.

HAND-OUT   Condition when change of server occurs. ('Hand-out' is also used as a marker's call to indicate that a change of hand has occurred.)

MATCH   The complete contest between two players commencing with the warm up and concluding when both players have left the court at the end of the final rally. (Covers broken ball rule.)

MATCH BALL   The state of the score when the server requires one point to win the match. ('Match ball' is also used as a marker's call.)

NOT UP   The expression used to indicate that a ball has not been struck in accordance with the rules. 'NOT UP' covers all returns which are not good and are neither 'DOWN' nor 'OUT' – with the exception of 'FAULTS' and 'FOOT-FAULTS'. ('Not up' is also used as a marker's call.)

OUT   The expression used to indicate that a ball has struck the out line or a wall above such line or the roof, or has passed over any part of the roof (e.g. cross bars). ('Out' is also used as a marker's call.)

OUT LINE   A continuous line comprising the front wall line, both side wall lines and the back wall line and marking the top boundaries of the court.

Note: When a court is constructed without provision of such a line i.e. the walls comprise only the area used for play, or without the provision of part of such a line (e.g. a glass back wall), and the ball in play strikes part of the horizontal top surface of such a wall and deflects back into court, such a ball is out. Because of the difficulty in ascertaining just where the ball strikes the wall, the decision as to whether such a ball is out should be made by observing the deflection back into court – an abnormal deflection indicating that the ball is out. This decision should be made in the normal manner by the marker, subject to appeal to the referee.

POINT   A unit of the scoring system. One point is added to a player's score when he is server and wins a stroke.

QUARTER (COURT)   One half of the back part of the court which has been divided into two equal parts by the half court line.

RALLY   Series of returns of the ball, comprising one or more such returns. A rally commences with a service and concludes when the ball ceases to be in play.

REASONABLE BACKSWING   The initial action used by a player in moving his racket away from his body as preparation prior to racket movement forward towards the ball for contact. A backswing is reasonable if it is not excessive. An excessive backswing is one in which the player's racket arm is extended towards a straight arm position and/or the racket is extended with the shaft approximately horizontal. The referee's decision on what constitutes a reasonable as distinct from excessive backswing is final.

REASONABLE FOLLOW-THROUGH The action used by a player in continuing the movement of his racket after it has contacted the ball. A follow-through is reasonable if it is not excessive. An excessive follow-through is one in which the player's racket arm is extended towards a straight arm position with the racket also extended with the shaft horizontal – particularly when the extended position is maintained for other than a momentary period of time. An excessive swing is also one in which the arm extended towards a straight position takes a wider arc than the continued line of flight of the ball, even though the racket shaft is in the correct vertical position. The referee's decision on what constitutes a reasonable versus excessive follow-through is final.

REFEREE (TOURNAMENT) Tournament referee is given overall responsibility for all marking and refereeing matters throughout the tournament including the appointment of officials to matches.

SERVICE The method by which the ball is put into play by the server to commence a rally.

SHORT LINE A line set out upon the floor parallel to and 5.49 metres (18 feet) from the front wall and extending the full width of the court.

STANDARD The description given to balls, rackets and courts that meet existing ISRF specifications.

STOP Expression used by the referee to stop play.

STRIKER The player whose turn it is to hit the ball after it has rebounded from the front wall, or who is in the process of hitting the ball, or who, up to the point of his return reaching the front wall, has just hit the ball.

STROKE The gain achieved by the player who wins a rally either in the normal course of play or on award by the referee and which results in either the scoring of a point or a change of hand.

TIME   The expression used by the referee to indicate that a period of time prescribed in the rules has elapsed.

TIN   Between the board and the floor for the full width of the court, the tin shall be constructed in such a manner as to make a distinctive noise when struck by the ball.

General Note 1   The use of the word 'SHALL' in the rules indicates compulsion and the lack of any alternative. The word 'MUST' indicates a required course of action with considerations to be taken into account if the action is not carried out. The word 'MAY' indicates the option of carrying out or not carrying out the action.

General Note 2   When the words 'HE' or 'HIM' are used in the rules, they shall be taken to mean 'SHE' and 'HER' as appropriate.

2 *Marker's Calls*

FAULT   See Rule 4.5b and 4.5c. The expression used to denote the service is a 'Fault'.

FOOT-FAULT   See Rule 4.5a The expression used to denote the service is a 'Foot-fault'.

NOT UP   The expression used to denote that a ball has not been served or returned above the board in accordance with the rules.

DOWN   The expression used to indicate that a ball has been struck against the tin or board.

ONE FAULT   The expression used to indicate the server is serving the second service.

OUT   The ball is out when it touches the front, sides or back of the court above the area prepared for play or passes over any cross bars or other part of the roof of the court. The lines delimiting such area, the lighting equipment and the roof are out.

3 Referee's Calls

STOP   Expression used by referee to stop play.

TIME   Expression used by referee to start play.

HALF-TIME   Expression used by referee when $2\frac{1}{2}$ minutes of the warm up have passed.

YES LET   Call made by referee when answering an appeal.

NO LET   Call made by referee when answering an appeal.

STROKE TO A   Call made by referee when answering an appeal.

STROKE TO B   Call made by referee when answering an appeal.

APPENDIX II: DIMENSIONS OF A
SINGLES COURT

Length 9·75 m (32 feet). Breadth 6·40 m (21 feet).

Height to upper edge of cut line on front wall 1·83 m (6 feet).

Height to lower edge of front-wall line 4·57m (15 feet).

Height to lower edge of back-wall line 2·13 m (7 feet).

Distance to nearest edge of short line from back wall 4·26 m (13 ft 10 in).

Height to upper edge of board from ground 0·48 m (19 in).

Thickness of board (flat or rounded at top) 12·5 to 25 mm ($\frac{1}{2}$ to 1 inch).

Height of side-wall line: The diagonal line joining the front-wall line and the back-wall line.

The service boxes shall be entirely enclosed on three sides within the court by lines, the short line forming the side nearest to the front wall, the side wall bounding the fourth side.

The internal dimensions of the service boxes shall be 1·60 m (5 feet 3 in).

All dimension in the court shall be measured, where practicable, from the junction of the floor and front wall at a height of 1 metre above the finished floor.

All lines of the court shall be 50 mm (2 inches) in width and all lines shall be coloured red. In respect of the outer boundary lines on the walls, it is suggested that the plaster should be so shaped as to produce a concave channel along such lines.

APPENDIX III : SPECIFICATION
OF A RACKET

1 *Dimensions*

a. Maximum length 685 mm (27 in)

b. Internal stringing

Maximum length 215 mm (8·5 in)

Maximum breadth 184 mm (7·25 in)

c. Framework of head

Maximum width across the face 14 mm (0·56 in)

Minimum width across the face 9 mm (0·36 in)

Maximum depth across the face 20 mm (0·81 in)

Minimum depth across the face 12 mm (0·47 in)

d. Shaft

Minimum thickness 9 mm (0·36 in)

e. Maximum weight (including stringing and bumper strip) 255 gms (9 ounces)

2 *Construction*

At all times, the head or shaft shall not contain edges with a radius of curvature less than 2 mm. Strings and string ends must be recessed within the racket head or, in cases where such recessing is impractical because of the racket material, or design, must be protected by a non-marking and securely attached bumper strip made of a flexible material, which cannot crease into sharp edges following abrasive contact with floors or walls.

Strings shall be gut, nylon or a substitute material, providing metal is not used. Only two layers of string shall be allowed and these shall be alternately interlaced to form an orthogonal array.

Note to Referees on Degradation   Rackets which have suffered damage so as to cause a potential hazard must not be used for play, unless the damaged region is repaired adhesively or by wound overlays, such that the damaged region becomes stronger than the material on either side of the damaged zone and has a smooth surface.

Manufacturers were given two years from 1 November 1983, to allow rackets made of wood, but which do not meet the new specification to clear the market. As from 1 November 1985, ALL rackets must meet the above specification.

APPENDIX IV: SPECIFICATION
FOR SQUASH RACKET BALLS

The ball must conform to the following:

1   It must weigh not less than 23·3 grammes and not more than 24·6 grammes (approximately 360–380 grains).

2   Its diameter must be not less than 39·5 mm and not more than 41·5 mm (approximately 1·56 to 1·63 inches).

3   It must have a surface finish which guarantees continuing correct rebound.

4   It must be of a type specifically approved for championship play by the ISRF.

5   Compression Specification:

i)   The ball is mounted in an apparatus and a load of 0·5 kgm is applied which deforms the ball slightly. Subsequent deformation in the test is measured from this datum.

ii)   An additional load of 2·4 kgm is applied and this deforms the ball further. The deformation from the datum position is recorded.

iii)   The deformation obtained in (ii) should be between 3 and 7 mm for balls of playing properties acceptable to the ISRF.

Organisers may specify regulations concerning players' clothing which must be complied with in their particular tournament or tournaments.

SRA note: For all events under the control of the SRA, players are required to wear white and/or light matching pastel clothing during the course of play. A coloured trim with a maximum width of 50 mm (2 inches) is permissible. Shoes should be predominantly white with only 20% of colour trim inclusive of sole, which must be non-marking. The maximum area for advertising is 50 mm² (2 inches²). Member countries of the ISRF have a limited discretion to allow advertising of a greater size to be worn for any other events under their control. The Referee's decision on compliance shall be final.

Note: Footwear is deemed clothing.

APPENDIX VI: CODE OF CONDUCT

The following offences may be subject to penalties under Rule 17 and/or disciplinary action:

1   A player who verbally or physically abuses his opponent, the marker, referee, officials, spectators or the sponsors.

2   A player who shows dissent to the marker, referee or officials, including foul or profane language and obscene or offensive gestures.

3   A player who abuses playing equipment or the court.

4   A player who fails to comply with the conditions of entry of a tournament including any rules with regard to clothing or advertising.

5   A player who, having entered a tournament or accepted an invitation to play, withdraws from the event or fails to attend.

6   A player who fails to complete a match.

7 A player who defaults from a tournament or event. The Disciplinary Committee may require evidence or proof of 'bona fide' injury, illness or other emergency situation.

8 A player who fails to make himself available to meet reasonable requests for interviews by the media.

9 A player who does not comply with the rules or spirit of the game.

10 A player guilty of any other unreasonable conduct which brings the game into disrepute.